Spice

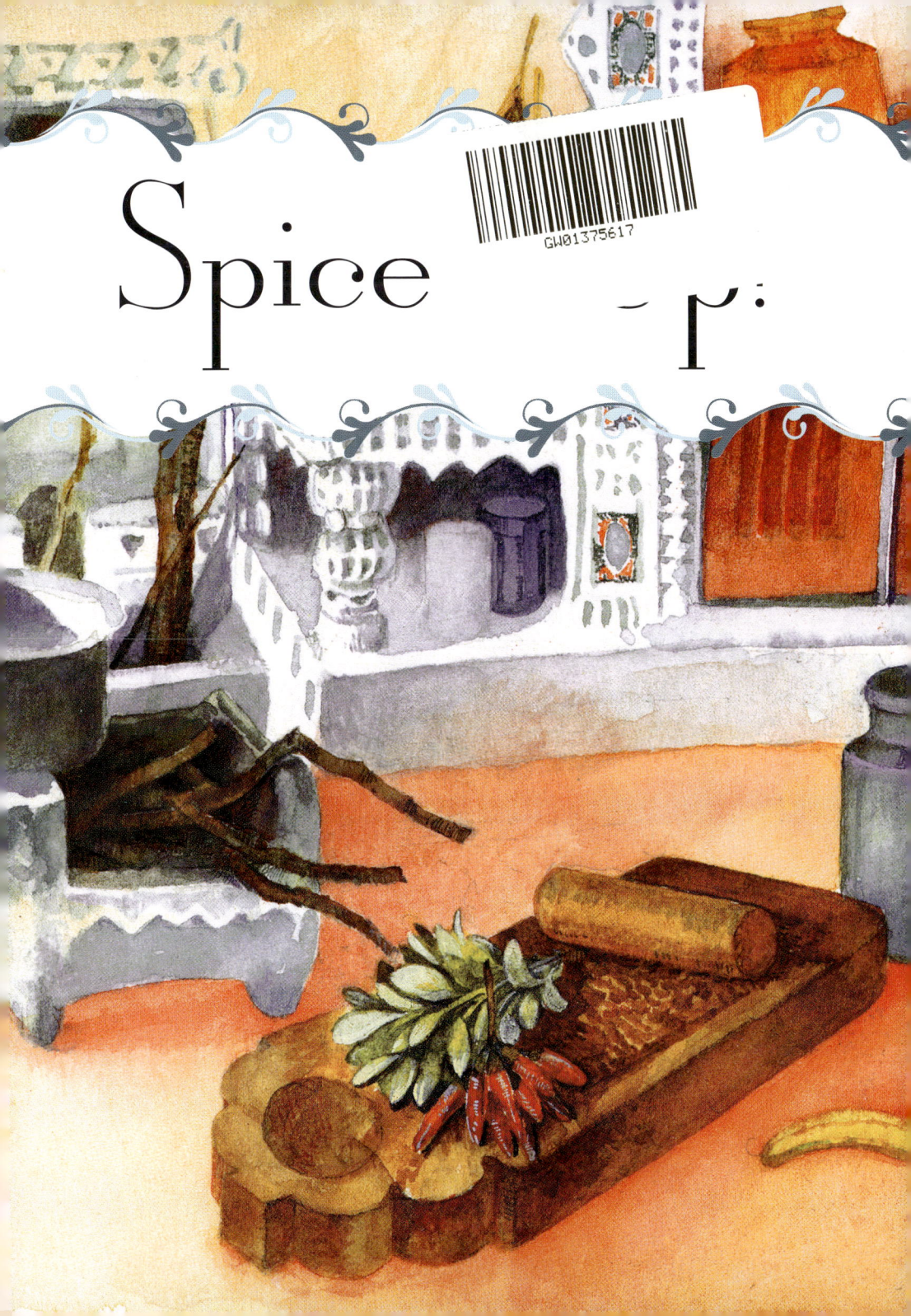

Contents

The Spice of Life	4
Spice and Mystery	6
The Pepper Hunt	8
The Spice Race	10
Islands of Spice	12
Hot! Hot! Hot!	
Pepper Confusion	14
Cowboys, Mexicans and Chilli	16
A Taste of India	18
Costly Spices	
Threads of Saffron	20
Beans of Vanilla	22
Salt and Pepper	24
Mountains of Salt	26
Fields of Colour	28
Glossary	30
Index	31
Research Starters	32

Features

TIME LINK

Long before Europeans discovered the Spice Islands the Bugis sailed to and from the islands. Discover more in **Pirates or Traders?** on page 13.

WORD BUILDER

Do you speak clearly? Test how well your tongue twists and spice up your vocabulary on page 15.

IN FOCUS

What gift would you treasure if you were getting married? Find out what spicy gift Indian brides were once given on page 19.

TRY THIS!

Follow the steps to make a delicious and nutritious spicy meal in a glass in **Make a Vanilla-Banana Smoothie** on page 23.

SITESEEING · PEOPLE & PLACES

How do people make curry powder?
Visit **www.infosteps.co.uk** for more about **SPICES**.

The Spice of Life

Fortunes have been made and nations discovered because of spices. The vibrant colours, inviting smells and exciting flavours of herbs and spices have been favourite ingredients in kitchens around the world for thousands of years.

Today when herbs and spices cost so little we can travel the world in our imagination while enjoying the vast variety of tastes and **aromas** of faraway lands.

Root

Bark

Flowers

Seed pods

Seeds

Leaves

IN FOCUS

Herbs and spices are fresh or dried parts of a plant. Spices generally grow in hot countries. They come from the bark, flowers, roots and seeds of plants.

Today many of the spices we buy have been ground into a fine powder. Sometimes spices such as cinnamon can be bought dried but not yet ground. A spice has a fresher flavour if it is ground as it is needed. The illustration on the title page shows a traditional spice grinder found in many kitchens in India.

Herbs usually come from the leaves of plants and are best used fresh. They grow in **temperate** climates.

5

Spice and Mystery

In ancient times herbs and spices were rare and precious products. For centuries Arabs controlled the trade of spices which came mainly from the **Far East**. The Arab traders kept their sources of supply a secret. They told tales of the dangers they faced in far-off lands to frighten away other traders.

The busy market of Baghdad was an important meeting place for traders from Asia and Europe. Spice traders brought pepper and cloves from India, cinnamon and nutmeg from Indonesia and ginger from China.

The ancient Persian Empire stretched as far as Egypt and India and included Baghdad in what is now Iraq.

In the Baghdad market traders would spend hours talking before agreeing on the best price for goods they were buying or selling.

In the days before refrigeration spices were used to disguise the taste of old meat. They were also used to make **incense**, perfume and medicine.

Arab traders sailed in ships called dhows. Today many dhows are still built in the same way they were hundreds of years ago.

Arab Trading Routes

EUROPE
EGYPT
AFRICA
Baghdad
PERSIA
INDIA
ASIA
CHINA
INDIAN OCEAN
INDONESIA

The Pepper Hunt

In medieval times Italy controlled the Mediterranean Sea and trade with Asia. The spice trade flowed through the Italian ports to the rest of Europe. Pepper was the largest import and was in high demand. The Italian traders demanded high prices.

Other European countries began searching for new routes to the spice-producing lands. They wanted to break the **monopoly** of the Italian traders. The hunt for pepper led to some of the greatest sea adventures in history.

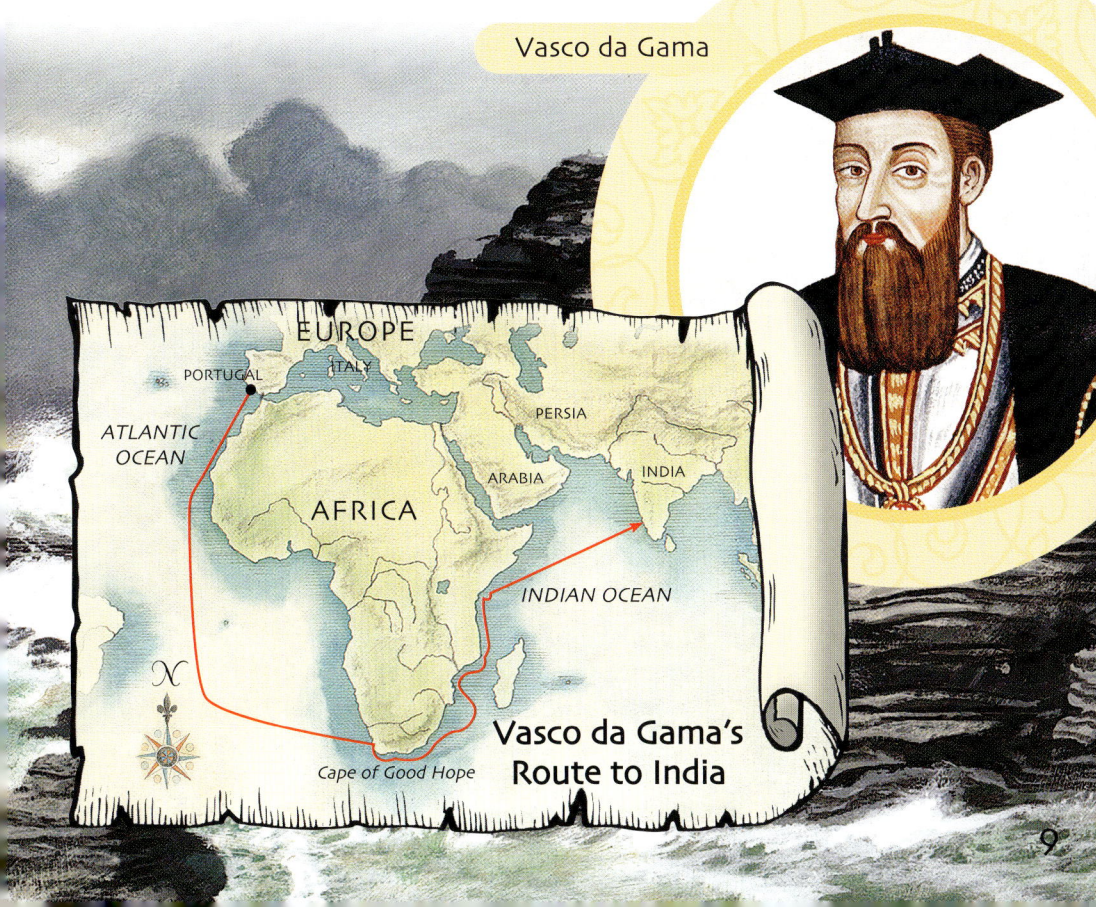

In 1497 the Portuguese sailor Vasco da Gama rounded the Cape of Good Hope and arrived in India in 1498. Spice traders were shocked to see the Portuguese ships and realized that their monopoly was now broken. Vasco da Gama returned to Portugal with his ships filled with pepper, cinnamon, ginger and jewels. Europeans realized that spice-producing lands could be reached by more than one sea route. The race to dominate the valuable spice business began.

Vasco da Gama

Vasco da Gama's Route to India

The Spice Race

From the 1500s through to the late 1700s Spain, Portugal, England and Holland all fought for control of the spice trade. Ferdinand Magellan's **circumnavigation** of Earth was Spain's attempt to find a shorter route to the Spice Islands in South-East Asia.

In 1600 Queen Elizabeth I of England set up the British East India Company and began to take control of India. By the late 1600s Holland had taken control of many of the Spice Islands. In 1780 the Dutch and English fought a war over the spice trade that destroyed Holland's power in the East.

The Dutch were determined to control the spice trade and fiercely protected entry into their islands. The French managed to get enough nutmeg (shown left), clove and cinnamon plants to begin growing spices in the French islands of the Indian Ocean and in French Guinea on the northern coast of South America.

In the 1500s and 1600s the country with the strongest navy was often able to control the countries where spices were grown. British navigators such as Sir Francis Drake (shown presenting a pearl necklace to Queen Elizabeth I) and the British navy's defeat of the Spanish Armada in 1588 made Britain a power at sea.

Islands of Spice

For thousands of years before European explorers arrived in South-East Asia the adventurous Bugis people were the masters of the sea. The Bugis built and sailed ships to carry spices and cargo to and from the 13,000 islands in the region. They traded with Arab and Chinese merchants who then started their journeys to the markets of Europe and China.

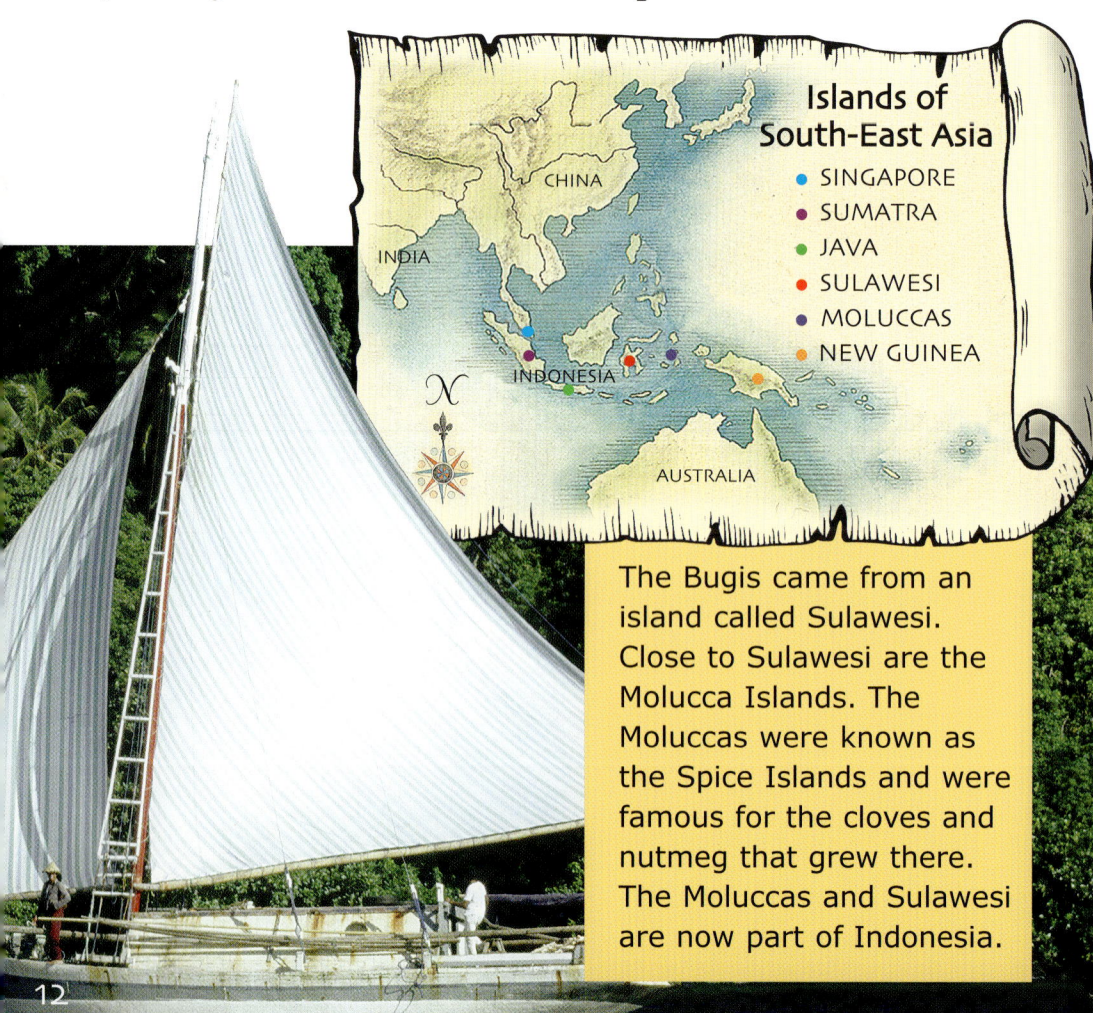

Islands of South-East Asia
- SINGAPORE
- SUMATRA
- JAVA
- SULAWESI
- MOLUCCAS
- NEW GUINEA

The Bugis came from an island called Sulawesi. Close to Sulawesi are the Molucca Islands. The Moluccas were known as the Spice Islands and were famous for the cloves and nutmeg that grew there. The Moluccas and Sulawesi are now part of Indonesia.

When the Dutch arrived in the region they cut off the traditional Bugis spice trade from Sulawesi to Java and they forced the Bugis to migrate to other areas. The Dutch introduced new crops such as tea, coffee, sugar and tobacco.

Pirates or Traders?

The Dutch fought to break the Bugis' trading links. They feared the Bugis sailors and called them pirates.

Today a large community of Bugis live in Singapore where many moved after violent disagreements with the Dutch in the early 1800s.

Bugis sailors continue to sail the seas from Singapore and Sumatra to the Moluccas and New Guinea. Their boats sail to tiny island ports and large mainland cities.

TIME LINK

Picking tea in Java

Hot! Hot! Hot!

Pepper Confusion

No one is really sure where the hottest spice, chilli, originally came from. Some people think the chilli first grew in the Amazon jungles. Seeds carried by the river and later by Aztec Indians spread throughout South and Central America and up to Mexico.

In 1492, six years before Vasco da Gama reached the East, Christopher Columbus set sail. He was hoping to find a direct western route to the Far East and to the home of pepper. Instead he arrived in the Americas. The closest thing he could find to pepper was the chilli. Columbus called the fiery vegetable "red pepper". Confusion over the use of the word *pepper* continues today.

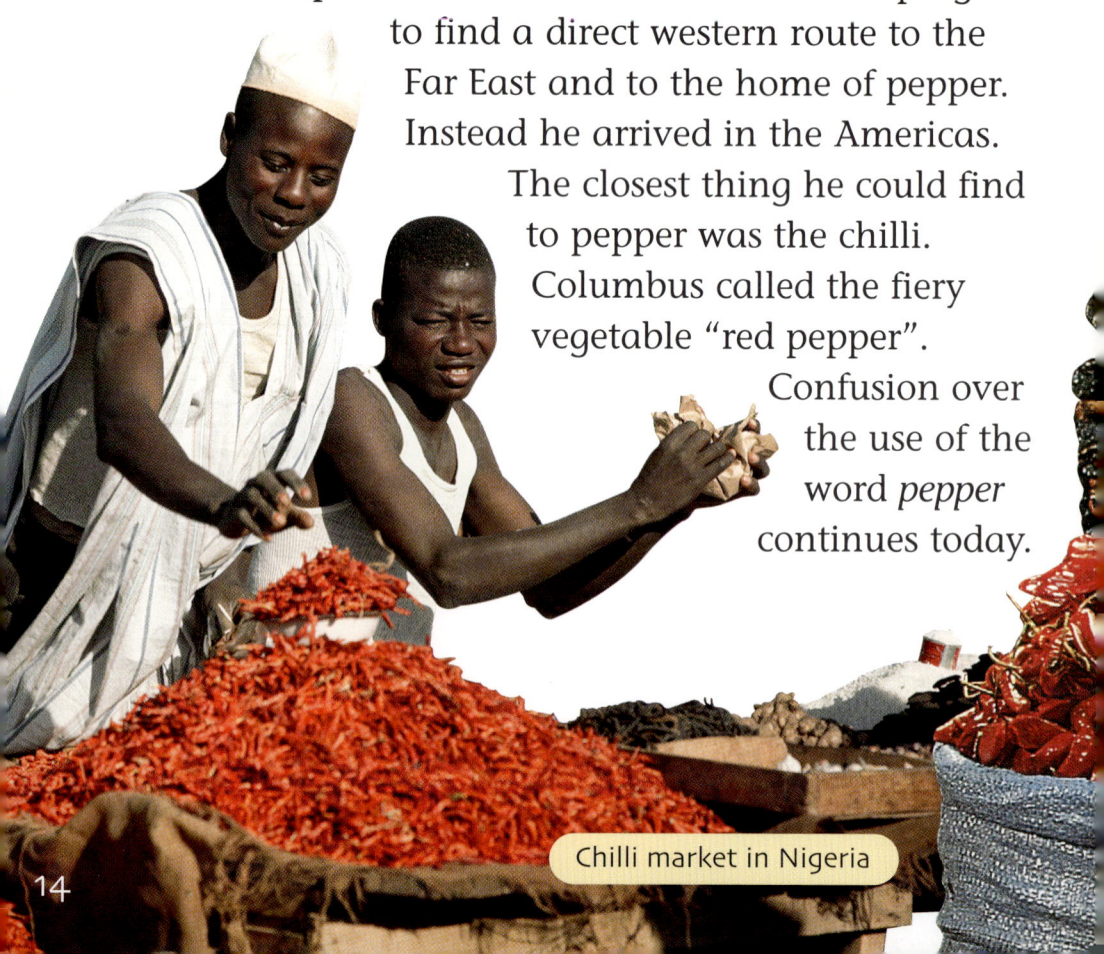

Chilli market in Nigeria

Peter Piper picked a peck of pickled peppers.

WORD BUILDER

This tongue-twisting rhyme is often used to practise clear speech. When a letter or sound at the beginning of a word is repeated in words close to each other, it is called alliteration. See if you can use alliteration to make a rhyme about another spice.

A peck is a unit of measure for foods such as spices, grains, fruits and vegetables. One peck equals about 38 cups. Peter picked a lot of peppers!

HOT CHILLIES

Cowboys, Mexicans and Chilli

If you think of Mexican food your tongue may tingle and your eyes may water. Mexican food can be hot! Mexican people use chillies in many different foods. They use them roasted, stewed, fried or simply fresh from the plant. There are more than 2,000 different varieties of the chilli pepper. They come in a wide range of colours, sizes, shapes and spiciness.

Mexican food was influenced when the Spanish colonists introduced spices and foods from Africa, South America, the Caribbean, France and the East to Mexico. Today a new **cuisine** known as Tex-Mex has become popular. It combines Mexican flavours with traditional Texan cowboy food. Chilli is an important ingredient in many Tex-Mex recipes.

It is a tradition in New Mexico to tie red chillies together into colourful long strings known as *ristras*. The *ristras* are hung near the entrances of homes as a symbol of friendliness.

Hot! Hot! Hot! continued

Texans take their chillies very seriously! Every year, "chilli cook-offs" are held to find the best recipes using chillies. Some say that the secret to a successful pot of chilli is to use a lot of very hot chilli peppers.

In the early 1800s English settlers in Texas ground together dried garlic, chilli peppers and oregano while trying to make a dish similar to the curries they had in their homeland. Thus ground chilli powder was invented. The early settlers could now make almost anything taste hot and spicy.

17

A Taste of India

The surprising colours, flavours, aromas and texture of the food of India help to show the many different ways that history and culture have shaped the nation. The different traditional and religious communities within India each have their own special cuisine. They use spices and prepare food in various ways.

Only a handful of spices are in fact native to India. These include cardamom, kari leaf and pepper. Some spices such as saffron were introduced to India by Persian traders over 4,000 years ago. Other herbs and spices were introduced over the centuries by immigrants. The ancient Romans brought coriander, cumin and fennel and the Portuguese brought chillies.

Long ago when a girl in an Indian village married she was given a *masaladani* or spice box. The covered container had several compartments containing spices for the bride to take to her new family and new home. Some boxes were carved from wood while others were made of gold and decorated with precious jewels.

Costly Spices

Threads of Saffron

Luckily the tiniest amount of saffron goes a long way. This is fortunate because it is the world's most expensive spice. Saffron is made from the **stigmas**, or threads, of the violet-coloured saffron flower. Each saffron flower has three delicate stigmas. It takes about 14,000 hand-picked stigmas to make just 25 grams of the deep orange spice!

Saffron has been harvested for thousands of years. Its delicate flavour and strong colour are in many Mediterranean and Asian dishes.

Only half a teaspoon of saffron threads have been used to give this rice a rich yellow colour. Cinnamon, cloves and cardamom pods are other spices that add flavour to this classic Indian dish called *Kesar Bhat*.

Stigmas, or threads

In India farmers **cultivate** fields of saffron flowers. Saffron is grown in many places including Spain, Turkey, China and Iran.

Stigma

Saffron flowers

Beans of Vanilla

Mmm . . . vanilla. Its aroma brings thoughts of delicious ice creams, cakes, biscuits and desserts. Vanilla is the fruit of a type of **orchid** plant and it grows in the form of a bean pod. Inside each bean are thousands of tiny black seeds.

Spanish explorers discovered vanilla in Mexico and brought it back to Europe where it quickly became popular. Vanilla orchids now grow in many other tropical countries. As with saffron the production of vanilla is complicated, making it expensive. Also like saffron a small amount has a large effect.

Vanilla pod

Costly Spices continued

Make a Vanilla-Banana Smoothie

This quick and easy drink not only tastes great, but also gives you lots of energy.

You Will Need:

- 1 cup orange juice
- 1 cup plain yoghurt
- 1 medium banana peeled and sliced
- 1 teaspoon vanilla essence (pure or imitation)

Method:

Have an adult help you blend all the ingredients until they're smooth. Makes two drinks.

Variations:

Add 1/2 cup fruit such as blueberries or strawberries. Sprinkle a pinch of nutmeg or cinnamon on top for an extra-sweet flavour.

Using vanilla beans, or pods, in food preparation can be time consuming. Liquid vanilla essence, commercially produced from the beans, is used instead. Imitation vanilla essence is also available. It is cheaper but has a similar flavour.

23

Salt and Pepper

Salt is not a spice or a herb, but it is commonly used to flavour food. Today salt is readily available, but in ancient times it was very precious. Salt was often traded for the same weight in gold. In many areas around the Mediterranean Sea cakes of salt were used for **currency**.

In ancient times salt was produced in the centre of the Sahara Desert in Africa, the largest desert in the world. Traders used camel caravans to carry heavy loads of salt to West Africa where the salt was traded for gold and other goods.

Pepper was a very popular and valuable spice in the Roman Empire. A single peppercorn dropped on the floor was hunted like a lost pearl. The main street on Rome's spice market was called *Via Piperatica*, Latin for "Pepper Street". When the Roman Empire fell the supply of pepper and many other spices dried up in Europe.

TIME LINK

The first salt and pepper shakers were made in the 1860s. Early shakers were really mills. Salt came in rock form and mills ground the salt and peppercorns into pieces. Salt and pepper shakers became popular in the 1940s when it became easier to make a variety of shapes and designs.

Mountains of Salt

Salt is necessary to both life and taste. A small amount of salt is important in our diet. Salt also brings out the flavour in food. Without it food can taste **bland**. Since ancient times salt has been used to preserve food. Today salt is mainly used in the chemical industry to manufacture things such as glass, paper, pesticides, antifreeze and soap. It is also often spread on roads to melt snow and ice.

The coastline of Vietnam is dotted with evaporation ponds and mountains of salt. China, France, India, Italy, Japan and Spain also produce solar salt.

Salt and Pepper continued

Most salt comes from salt mines and the sea. Rock salt is mined from underground deposits formed by the evaporation of oceans millions of years ago. Solar salt is formed by evaporating sea water. This is the oldest method of harvesting salt and requires a hot dry climate.

WORD BUILDER

Salt **seasons** language as well as food. A person described as "the salt of the Earth" is seen as being honest and hard working. To "take it with a grain of salt" means to not believe everything you are told because some of it may not be true. To "rub salt into the wound" means to make a situation worse. To "salt away" your money means to save a little money regularly.

Underground salt deposits are found on every continent. Most of the salt mined in Canada comes from underground deposits in the south-western provinces of Canada. In winter months large quantities of salt are used to melt snow on roads in Canada.

Fields of Colour

Mustard is one of the oldest spices and is one of the world's most popular seasonings. The Chinese have grown mustard for 3,000 years. Ancient Egyptians popped mustard seeds into their mouths while chewing meat. The ancient Greeks and Romans used it as an everyday spice to flavour food.

Dijon, France has been an important centre for mustard production since the 1200s. The French consider mustard the **condiment** of kings. Dijon mustard is made from ground mustard seeds blended with vinegar, cloves, cinnamon and other herbs and spices.

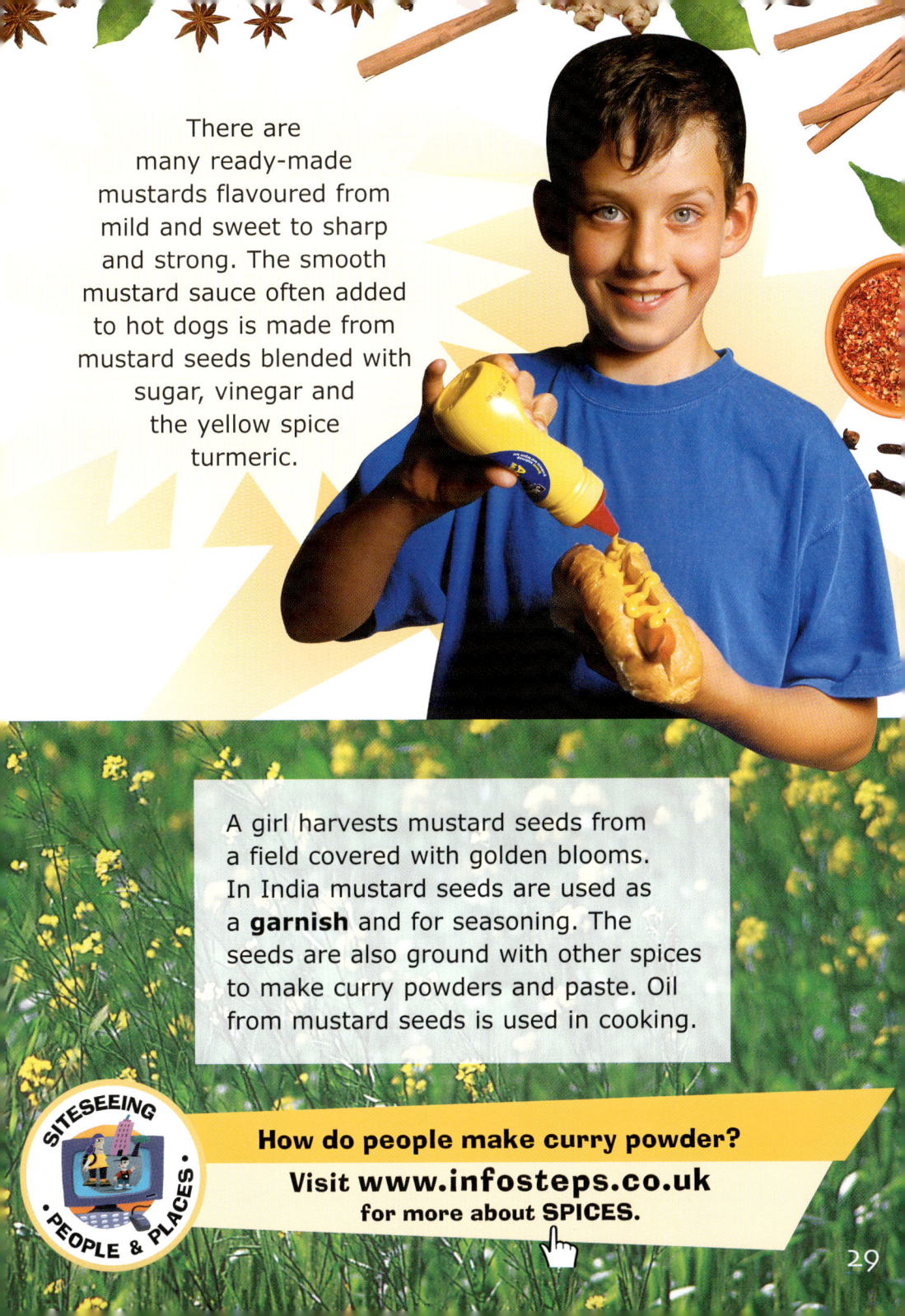

There are many ready-made mustards flavoured from mild and sweet to sharp and strong. The smooth mustard sauce often added to hot dogs is made from mustard seeds blended with sugar, vinegar and the yellow spice turmeric.

A girl harvests mustard seeds from a field covered with golden blooms. In India mustard seeds are used as a **garnish** and for seasoning. The seeds are also ground with other spices to make curry powders and paste. Oil from mustard seeds is used in cooking.

How do people make curry powder?
Visit www.infosteps.co.uk
for more about SPICES.

Glossary

aroma – a smell that is usually pleasant

bland – mild and plain in flavour

circumnavigation – sailing all the way around

condiment – a substance that is used to add flavour to food. Herbs and spices are condiments.

cuisine – a style or way of cooking or presenting food

cultivate – to grow and care for plants

currency – the money used in a country

Far East – the countries of east Asia including Indonesia, Malaysia, Singapore, Vietnam, China and Japan

garnish – to decorate food with small amounts of other food, herbs or spices to make it look or taste better

incense – a substance that gives off a sweet smell when it is burned

monopoly – complete control of a service or product in a place by a single person or company. A company that has a monopoly has no competition.

orchid – a plant with colourful and unusually shaped flowers

season – add to or change the flavour of food with herbs, salt or spices

stigma – the part of a flower that receives pollen during pollination

temperate – a climate that is neither very hot nor very cold. The United States, southern Australia and New Zealand all have temperate climates.

Index

Africa	7, 9, 16, 24
Americas, the	14, 16
Asia	6–8, 10, 12–13, 20
Bugis people	12–13
China	6–7, 12, 21, 26, 28
Columbus, Christopher	14
Drake, Sir Francis	11
Egypt	6–7, 28
England	10–11, 17
Europe	6–9, 12, 22, 25
France	10, 16, 26, 28
Gama, Vasco da	9, 14
Holland	10, 13
India	5–7, 9–10, 12, 18–19, 21, 26, 29
Italy	8–9, 26
Magellan, Ferdinand	10
Mexico	14, 16, 22
Persia	6–7, 9, 18
Portugal	9–10, 18
Romans	18, 25, 28
Spain	10–11, 16, 21, 26
Spice Islands	10, 12

31

Research Starters

1 There are many different spices in the world. Think of a spice not described in this book. What does it look and taste like? Where does it grow today? How is it used with food? Does it have other uses?

2 Choose a country, not your own, that grows and exports spices. Locate the country on a map of the world. Find out about other products that this country exports. What is the population of the country and what languages do the people speak? What other interesting facts about this country can you find?

3 Interview an adult you know who enjoys cooking. Which herbs and spices does he or she use? What is his or her favourite herb or spice? Why? In which recipes is this herb or spice used?

4 Find out all you can about the history of serving salt and pepper and the materials used to make shakers. Design a set of shakers unlike any you've seen.